BEYOND THE
RAINBOW

ABOUT THE COVER

During the past few years, I have developed an interest in photography. As I was writing the book, I had several pictures of rainbows as possible cover photos, but none was quite suitable. I had prayed that God would send me an image I could use.

Driving home from a neighbouring town one early evening, I noticed a beautiful rainbow in the distance. I had prayed for this moment but I could only keep driving and hope that my husband had seen the sky and was taking pictures.

After pulling into our driveway, I ran past him in the garage on my way to the basement.

"Where is the camera?" I called from halfway down the stairs. I was sure I had left it on the desk.

"I have it here," he called back. "I have been taking pictures of the double rainbow."

"Thank you, Lord," I replied on my way back to the garage, "and thank you, Patrick."

BEYOND THE RAINBOW

God's Hand at Work

Blanche J. Brideau

Edited by Peggy Klem

iUniverse, Inc.
Bloomington

BEYOND THE RAINBOW
GOD'S HAND AT WORK

iUniverse books may be ordered through booksellers or by contacting:

iUniverse
1663 Liberty Drive
Bloomington, IN 47403
www.iuniverse.com
1-800-Authors (1-800-288-4677)

ISBN: 978-1-4620-4684-3 (sc)
ISBN: 978-1-4620-4685-0 (ebk)

Printed in the United States of America

iUniverse rev. date: 09/13/2011

Grandma and Grandpa Boudreau

CONTENTS

Dedication ix

Acknowledgments xi

Introduction..xiii

    1. The Power of Prayer 1

    2. A Little Boy's Wish..9

    3. Blessings along the Way....................................18

    4. A Woman of Courage.......................................27

    5. A Winter Rose..37

    6. My Christmas Present 41

    7. A Special Rainbow 50

    8. The Power of Love 54

    9. The Gift..60

  10. Full Circle..65

  11. Sophie and Her Courageous Battle
       with Cancer Saying Goodbye 69

  12. Remember Me 74

In Conclusion 79

About The Author..81

DEDICATION

This collection of short stories is dedicated to the memory of my grandfather, Marcel Boudreau, and to my parents, George and Rosalie Brideau. Grandpa was tall and slender, a humble man with a quiet demeanour that exuded goodness. A man of honour and the spiritual leader of our family, Grandpa lived his life according to the teachings of the Bible. Although I never knew him well, he had a great influence on my life. It was through his incredible faith and trust in God that we came to understand the importance and the power of prayer in our lives.

After Grandma passed away, Grandpa left the farm and moved to Ontario with his eldest son, Harry. Brothers Don, Aurel, and Edward had already made the move. We did not see him often after that, but if I closed my eyes, I could still smell the sweet aroma of his pipe tobacco. He was an avid gardener who enjoyed planting and working in his vegetable garden until he was in his late eighties. When he was ninety, he returned to the east and moved in with my parents, where he would live out the remainder of his life. I was a teenager then and, like most teens, was more absorbed in my own life. I sure wish I had spent more time getting to know him.

Most of what I knew about my grandparents I learned from my mother. She was a tall and elegant woman, a true lady in every sense, who had inherited many of her father's attributes. She was not able to attend school after the sixth grade because of her mother's illness, but she was wise beyond what conventional schooling might have taught her.

Our father left home when he was eleven years old. He had no formal education and could barely write his name, but he worked hard to provide for his family. He was a strong man who spent his life in lumber camps, where he developed a respect for and a love of horses. I have fond memories of coming out of school on a stormy winter day to find Dad waiting for us with horse and sleigh.

Every day I appreciate the lessons that I learned while growing up in a large family. The sense of gratitude for what I have and what I can share brings me great joy. Although my parents endured many struggles and hardships, they had incredible resilience. It was through their faith in God and the love for their children that they continued to trudge forward and overcome many trials.

Mom and Dad, I thank you both for the values that I hold dear and try to live by each day.

ACKNOWLEDGMENTS

It is with a grateful heart that I give thanks to the Creator for helping me translate onto paper the stories that have opened my eyes to the love of God and the power of prayer. To the stranger who told me thirteen years ago that I should write the first story because it needed telling—thank you!

Three years ago, my son, Nelson, presented me with a gift. It consisted of a notebook, a pen, a black box, and a silver plaque with the engraved words "I will write a book." Two weeks earlier, I had asked him what he thought about my idea of writing a book. Now he had written, "Mom, I know you can, so write to your heart's content. Put some ideas in this notebook, and before you know it, your book will come to life, all by itself. I cannot wait to see the finished copy. Love you lots, Nelson." Thank you, son, for your thoughtfulness. Encouraged by these comments, for my Lenten journey that year I committed to write every day. So I prayed and I wrote, prayed some more and wrote still more, until I had the stories on paper.

A few days later, my husband noticed an advertisement for a creative writing course in our community and immediately signed me up. Patrick, I will be forever grateful for your love and support.

To Susan, Jean, Cindy, Dawn, and Dorothy for sharing your stories and trusting me to put them down on paper, I thank you. To Mackenzie and Grace, two beautiful little girls who bring a lot of joy to my life, love from Grandma BJ.

I also want to pay tribute to Mom Williams who passed away on July 22. She was a gentle woman who said very little yet taught me so much. Thank you for welcoming me into your home and into your heart. You will be greatly missed.

To all the wonderful people in my life for your encouragement and enthusiasm, my sincere thanks and love to each one of you.

To my siblings Marie, Evelyn, Tina, Andrew, Edna, Roy, Jackie, Theresa, and Edward for your love and support throughout the years, thank you. Mom and Dad would be happy and proud that we are so closely connected. To Gerard, who died as an infant: I look forward to meeting you someday. Special thanks to my late brother, Nelson, for opening my mind and heart to a life *Beyond the Rainbow*.

INTRODUCTION

This book contains a collection of compelling, heartwarming short stories that may make you cry but will definitely be thought-provoking. They are based on the lives of real people, and I feel blessed to have a special connection to each one of them.

Some of the stories are from my childhood memories and some have been passed down to me by my mother. Others are experiences that involve friends, though some names have been changed. These stories underline not only the power of faith and prayer but also the wonderful results of listening to what some may define as intuition. This may come to you as a gentle whisper, a nudge, or a big jolt. Any impact you may have on someone else will depend on whether you learn to recognize and respond to this inner voice.

I believe that angels walk among us every day. I am grateful that they watch over me as I stumble along on my life's journey. Each story deals with faith, hope, and courage in a world filled with pain, injustice, and grief. The common thread through all of them is love. They tell about a mother's and a father's love for their children, a sister's love for her sibling, or a stranger's love for a hungry child. All of these stories have made me feel loved beyond my understanding, and they reflect beyond doubt the Father's love for each one of us.

My grandfather's farm.

CHAPTER ONE

The Power of Prayer

Front, L-R: Tina, age 5, Andrew, age 4
Top: Evelyn, age 8, Marie, age 9

As a young child, I loved listening to Mom tell stories that had greatly touched her life and affirmed her belief in a loving God. The following is one of these stories.

1

Spring of 1946 was a welcome sight after the long, cold winter. Mom, pregnant with her fourth child, was still trying to deal with the loss of our older brother Gerard to crib death the year before. It had been a terrible shock for our parents, and Dad's hopes and dreams for his firstborn son had vanished that day.

Our two sisters, Evelyn and Marie, age three and four, were excited about a new baby. This child would fill our home with the joy that comes with new life. Early in her pregnancy, Mom had had an accident when our horse reared up in front of her. She had tripped and landed hard on a tree stump. From that moment on, she had concerns for the child she was carrying.

Living in a remote part of northern New Brunswick had its drawbacks. It meant that our mother, like other pregnant women who were soon to deliver, would have to leave home a month before her due date. When it was time for Mom to leave home, Evelyn and Marie were placed in the care of our Aunt Lucy, who was also looking after our ailing grandmother

It was a twenty-five mile journey to the nearest hospital. The only way out was by way of a pump trolley on the rails. The trolley made the trip to town twice a week so families could pick up needed supplies.

While Mom was waiting at her sister Evelyn's home to have the baby, her mother passed away, but because she was so close to her due date, she was unable to return home for the funeral.

On March 28, 1946, Mom gave birth to a tiny baby girl. To our parents' disbelief, Antonia, later nicknamed Tina, was born with a condition they would come to know as dwarfism. The doctor who delivered Tina did not expect her to survive; therefore, the priest was called, and she was baptized shortly after her birth. She was born with a large cleft palate, the first of many concerns for our parents. Our mother's attempts at both breastfeeding and bottle-feeding her newborn were unsuccessful. Because of her cleft, Tina was unable to create suction to draw the milk from the nipple. The medical staff, certain that she would die, suggested to our parents that they leave her at the hospital. Against their advice, Mom and Dad bundled up their tiny baby and headed home. Our mother was both devastated by Antonia's problems and heartbroken to know that Grandma would not be there to provide moral support and the advice for which we often look to our mothers when faced with difficulties.

Home at the time was the little red house behind Grandpa's farm. There was no electricity or indoor plumbing, and Dad had to get the water from our grandfather's well and transport it to our house by horse and buggy. After Mom's many attempts to feed her baby from a bottle, she improvised by using a medicine dropper. It took three hours to get one ounce of milk into her tiny baby. Although it was very time-consuming, it worked. Tina was the size of a small doll, weighing approximately two pounds, and she fit perfectly into a shoebox. She had a head full of brown hair that framed her little round face and beautiful eyes. To keep her body warm during the day, she was placed on the open oven door of the old cook stove. Our mother ordered a bottle of rubbing oil from the Sears catalogue. After Tina's bath, she would apply the oil to her tiny arms and legs in the hope that it would help in the development of her muscles and stimulate her growth. Under our parents' loving care, their little girl soon began to flourish. Six months later when the doctor saw her, he could not believe his eyes. He had not expected her to live days, let alone months.

Our parents would have many concerns about Tina's development. They knew by the way her legs were positioned that she would have difficulty moving around, let alone walking. Having a family with a special-needs child, and living in a remote area, Mom would have to be physiotherapist, nutritionist, and speech therapist as well as performing all the daily duties that go along with being a parent. Tina needed extra attention, but our mother had an amazing capacity to fill all those roles and still find the time to love and nurture the remainder of her children. Mom was often on her own to keep the house warm and to care for the children, as Dad had to spend most of his time working in the forest cutting wood, which was sent down to the paper mill by way of the river.

There were twelve families in our small community, and three of those families were our relatives, who provided some support when Dad was at work. The power plant employed most of the people in the area, with the exception of Grandpa, who tried to make a living on the land.

Although Tina was not able to walk, she learned the art of crawling. From a sitting position, she would swing one leg over the other, propelling herself forward. She managed to get around quite well, but how would she cope at school? Mom could not be there to carry her around, and besides, she had two more babies at home who needed her care. She knew that for Tina to have any chance of going to school she would need to walk.

The month of May was a very special time for our family. I have wonderful memories of being a young child accompanying our mother into the forest around the house, where we would gather mayflowers and moss. Each spring we would pick the tiny blue flowers that Mom would use to decorate the statue of Mary. Each night after supper, our family, like many other Roman Catholic families, would gather and recite the rosary. Sometimes we would be outdoors playing, but when our parents called we headed home. It was time to give thanks for the blessings of the day. It was an important time for us as a family, as we learned and understood the value and importance of prayer.

Our parents had a strong devotion to Mary. This particular May, Tina was four and still not walking. Therefore, our mother decided that she would say a novena to Mary, asking her to intercede with the Father in the hope of obtaining a miracle. A novena is a prayer repeated for nine consecutive days requesting a special grace, and Mom's request was that Tina would learn to walk. She knew it would take a miracle.

Mom was six months pregnant at the time with her seventh child. Each afternoon while our older sisters looked after my brother and me, she would gather Tina in her arms and walk the half mile to our little country church nestled in the pines. The building by today's standards would be the equivalent of a tiny chapel. The doors were always open to people as a refuge from the daily struggles they faced. Pine boards covered the floors, and the walls were of painted plywood. It was sparsely furnished with a very modest altar and seating for approximately twenty-five people. Above the altar there was a large wooden cross holding a figure of our crucified Lord. Statues of Mary and Joseph were to His right and to His left. With Tina in her arms, Mom would enter the church and kneel before the statue of Mary. Then, with her heart filled with love for her child, she would pray. Day after day she carried Tina to the little church, and day after day she made the same petition as she continued the novena. Because May was the time dedicated to Mary, Mom recited the novena throughout the month. Tina herself has vivid memories that are very special to her of the times that our mother carried her to church in her arms.

When Mom returned home on the last day of May, as she did most days, she placed Tina on a blanket in the yard with her siblings, but this day she would remember as the day that God answered her prayers for her child. After a short time, Tina left the security and comfort of her blanket and crawled approximately ten feet to the corner of the house. She then proceeded to pull herself up, using her hands and the building to get her balance, and then she slowly inched her way along the house. She did this for several days until she found the courage to let go. According to Mom, Tina fell numerous times, but it did not stop her from trying repeatedly until she mastered the art of walking. Although her gait was unusual, with her tiny feet pointing outward, she would propel herself forward using the same principle that had enabled her to crawl.

Because of our mother's strong belief in the power of prayer and her dedication to Mary, her little girl was finally able to walk. Our parents were so happy for Tina, as they watched in awe the wonderful miracle that had taken place. It meant that Tina would be able to enjoy the freedom and independence that she for many years had observed in her younger siblings.

At the age of six, Tina stood twenty-four inches tall, and the school refused to accept her because of her size. The next year she was still the same size, but Mom insisted that Tina be allowed to attend. On her first day of school, our older sisters pushed her along in a stroller. Tina found it embarrassing, and the following day she refused to ride. It was too far for her to walk, so Marie and Evelyn took turns carrying her on their shoulders until there was enough snow on the ground for a toboggan.

Through the years, Tina's education was often interrupted by her many health concerns. Because of her cleft, Tina had difficulty speaking clearly, and although the family could understand what she was saying, it was often a challenge for strangers. Due to her physical disabilities, many people thought that she was also mentally challenged. In later years, she would have surgery in an attempt to repair the cleft, but the procedure was unsuccessful.

When Tina was in her pre-teens, our parents made numerous trips to the hospital where she underwent a barrage of X-rays and assessments to see if anything could be done to improve her gait. Her feet were facing outward and her heels faced each other. Orthopaedic specialists suggested to our parents that if her legs were broken, they could be straightened and put in casts. There were no guarantees that the procedure would work; therefore, our parents would not take the risk. Tina would carry on as usual.

Tina, being the fourth eldest in a family of twelve siblings, was well settled in when the rest of us arrived. To the younger members of the family she was just another sibling and treated no differently. In fact, we made sure she did her share of the chores, even if it meant she had to stand on a chair to wash the dishes.

Her upbringing, I am certain, gave our big "little" sister the strength and courage she needed to face her many challenges. Tina grew up in a large, loving family who accepted her for the wonderful person she is. She was a source of strength to our mother and is now the centre of our family. She is the one who keeps us all connected. Her most precious asset is her kind and forgiving nature, which I am sure comes from her having lived in a world filled with so much adversity. In her late twenties, she headed to Ontario, Canada, where she continues to live an independent and productive life. Now in her early sixties, Tina stands three feet four inches, and she is an inspiration to all who meet her.

Note: The rosary is a beautiful meditative prayer on the life of Jesus and His mother, Mary. It began in the Middle Ages as a way of praying the 150 Psalms. The mysteries were created to help people ponder each day the main events of Jesus's life. By meditating on the mysteries, we pray that they will lead us to a deeper understanding of who Jesus is and what His life means.

Source: *Scarboro Missions* magazine, May–June 2009 edition.

CHAPTER TWO

A Little Boy's Wish

Nelson age 3

In the summer of 1959, our parents moved us to a new home, in a rural farming community approximately forty miles from where we had spent the early part of our childhood. Dad was struggling to find work as a logger and had accepted a job at the nearest paper mill. They were hopeful for a brighter future.

It had been an exciting adventure; Mom made sure of that. I loved the beautiful yellow clapboard farmhouse that Dad had rented from Mom's distant cousin. We were still nine children at home, so sharing a room with one sibling instead of finding ourselves three or four to a bed was a luxury we had never known.

Because there were many hungry mouths to feed, Dad decided to supplement the groceries by planting a large garden. Our job as children was to keep the potato bugs off the plants and the weeds at bay. We did not like it much, but we were still expected to do our part. If there was any lesson that our parents taught us, it was the importance of being united as a family. That included everything from praying to playtime.

That first summer we spent exploring our new surroundings. A lovely creek ran beside the house, and a beautiful apple orchard graced the property. It provided us with hours of enjoyment trying to find the biggest and juiciest fruit. Nelson and Roy, who were five and seven at the time, had great fun pushing a battered pram up and down the driveway to the main road. The competition was always about who could run the fastest. We had large fields in which to play, not to mention the old barn where Dad kept his prize Clydesdale horses. We managed to entertain ourselves well that summer, although we missed our extended family.

Fall was fast approaching, which meant that Andrew and I would be attending the junior high school a short bus ride away. The younger siblings would have a twenty-minute walk to the little red schoolhouse. If anyone looked forward to September, it was our mother, even though there were still four younger siblings at home.

The long, cold winter ahead would prove to be a very difficult time financially for our parents. It took every cent that Dad made to keep us warm and fed. On cold nights, our mother would go from bed to bed covering us with our winter coats for added warmth. I know Marie and Evelyn, who worked outside the home, often gave a portion of their income to help our parents with the expenses. We were sheltered from the worries that our parents faced that winter, although

I do remember some weird concoctions like fried lard, flour, and water that we had to eat on occasion. As children, we had a great time skating on the frozen creek just outside our door. By then we were happy with our new friends and had settled in quite nicely.

With the first signs of spring came the lovely apple blossoms, and for our parents the burdens of winter were slowly diminished with the hopes that life might get a little easier.

Andrew and I were preparing for confirmation that spring. Our brother Nelson, who was five years old at the time, also wanted to make his "confirbation," as he pronounced it. Mom had to reassure him that when he reached the age of ten, the bishop would return to our church and confirm all the children in his age group, but this did not prevent him from inquiring about it several more times.

Mom had told us that we would receive the gifts of the Holy Spirit, and although we were not sure what that meant, we were very excited.

When the day finally arrived, our parents and all of our siblings filled our two assigned pews in the church. It was a special day for the family, a rather grand ceremony, different from the regular church service. The bishop, decked in his brightly coloured robe, ceremonial hat, and staff, added a festive air to the occasion.

Sundays were also special in our home, in particular for our little brother Nelson, who loved to go to church. He would come down the stairs dressed in the clothes that he had placed neatly in his section of the dresser the previous week. He especially loved a little brown sweater that matched those big brown eyes of his. When the family returned home from the service, he would not have to be told to change into play

11

clothes. He kept a special outfit for his special day. It was his little routine.

In those days, when Dad was working on a Sunday, those of us big enough to walk the two miles to church would head out in hopes that a kind neighbour would pick us up. Mom would have to stay behind with the younger children.

When summer finally arrived, it meant the end of schoolwork, but it was back to picking potato bugs and tending to the weeds. Regardless, we were happy to play and enjoy the long days with Mom and with Dad when he was not at the mill.

I especially remember one of those days when most of us were gathered around the table in anticipation of the cookies that our mother would soon be taking out of the oven. It was the delicious smell of molasses that had drawn us to the kitchen in the first place. We had just come in from the hot sun, when our little brother Nelson, who was sitting next to me, asked our mother what she would do when he died.

"Do not talk like that!" she said.

To this he replied, "You will see, Mommy." On another occasion, we were outside playing when he gazed into the sky and said, "I am going there soon," and then he gave a little laugh.

Death was not a subject that was often discussed in our home, except on the odd occasion when Nelson brought it up. In later years, we would come to some understanding of the special little boy that he was.

September was just around the corner; we would once again be heading back to school, and this year Nelson would be joining us. He had turned six in April, and he was ready and had been anticipating this day with great excitement. He would finally be able to see inside the little red schoolhouse and sit at his own desk! Our mother wondered how he would cope in a new environment. He was an extremely shy little boy who would often escape to the security of his bedroom when strangers came to our door. I remember trying to coax him out from under the bed when our parents wanted to introduce us to someone.

Thursday was the first day of school for the younger kids, and Mom was excited for Nelson as he headed out the door accompanied by three of his older siblings. She anxiously awaited his return, but when he came in the house the excitement he felt was somewhat overshadowed by his complaint of a bellyache. Mom attributed it to a combination of his first day of school and his shy personality. However, by late afternoon he was feeling so ill that our father and sister Evelyn took him to the local hospital, about twenty miles from our home, where he was admitted for observation. Dad left Nelson in the care of the doctor and nurses and returned to the family. Our parents were certain that with the help of antibiotics their little boy would soon be home and back in school. The next day he was diagnosed with the poliovirus. They were shocked, but they kept their concerns to themselves. We, along with many other children in the community, had not been vaccinated.

Friday morning Mom and Dad were told that the virus had attacked the muscles in Nelson's chest, making it difficult for him to breathe; they remained hopeful that he would recover.

The next evening the call came for Mom to return to the hospital, because Nelson's condition had worsened. Her shoulders were slumped as she made her way down the long corridor. *Dear God*, she prayed, *Please do not let my little boy die*. She could hear footsteps coming toward her. When she raised her head, she came face to face with the local bishop. For a brief moment, she wondered what he was doing in the hospital on a Saturday night, and then she remembered her little boy's wish. They spoke briefly, and Mom told the bishop that her son was very ill and asked if he could be confirmed.

The bishop kindly followed our mother into Nelson's room. Dad was already there, having gone straight from work. In the quiet evening, with Mom and Dad at his side, our dear little brother was granted his wish and received the gifts of the Holy Spirit through the sacrament of confirmation. Our parents sat by his bedside comforting him as they silently prayed for a cure. They would return home later that evening to tend to the rest of the children and get some much-needed sleep.

Sunday morning, the neighbour who had the only telephone in the area came with a message from the hospital that Nelson had passed away. About five minutes later, a conflicting message arrived that they should come to the hospital because his condition was critical. Our frantic parents rushed to the hospital, but Mom never made it to his room. Emotionally exhausted, she collapsed into a chair beside the elevator. Dad went on to Nelson's room and found him curled up in his hospital bed. He appeared to have been gazing into the corner of his room as though he had seen something. The shy little smile with which we were all so familiar was still present on his angelic face. He was gone. Devastated, our parents were later told that if Nelson had lived, he would have had to spend the rest of his life in an iron lung. Mom and Dad were grateful for God's mercy. Our life as we knew it would undergo many changes as our parents tried to move forward.

In the midst of all their grief, our parents were instructed by the health authorities to destroy everything that Nelson had been in contact with. His school desk that he had occupied for three short hours was removed and burned. All his clothing and bedding would also have to be destroyed. With the help of our older siblings, the entire household contents had to be sterilized.

I walked outside the next morning and saw Mom standing on the porch. I watched as she lifted item after item of Nelson's clothing from the pile she had placed beside her. She held each piece gently before placing it into a burning barrel. The last item she picked up was the little brown sweater he had often worn to church. She could not bring herself to destroy it. She would need something tangible to comfort her, so, after washing it several times she then tucked it into her corner of the dresser. It would become a bittersweet reminder of the precious child she had lost.

I wandered into the barn that afternoon and found my father crouched in a corner, crying, his hands covering his tearstained face. When he saw me, he quickly got up, trying to hide his grief.

The health authorities had placed our home under quarantine, and the kitchen became the examining room. The doctor arrived, and one by one we were lifted onto the old pine table and checked for signs of the virus. Each time the doctor examined one of us and said that we were okay, our parents breathed a sigh of relief.

When it was Roy's turn, he complained of a sore leg. Because of his complaint and the fact that the boys shared a bed, Roy was immediately taken from us and sent to a hospital located about two and a half hours from our home. He was eight years old at the time, and our mother would have to stay behind with the remainder of the children. The next day, the doctor called with the devastating news that Roy was also infected.

We would find out later that the virus had attacked the muscles on the right side of his body, leaving him with some paralysis, but he would survive. He had to be away from home for approximately six months, and our parents could only manage to make the trip to see him twice. Roy has memories of waking up in a room with a priest and nuns praying over him. When he looked up, he saw Mom and Dad looking in through a small window in the door. He had to spend several weeks in quarantine, and then he faced months in rehabilitation. I look at him today, and it saddens me to think of the torment he must have had to endure. The loss of his brother, the fear of his own death, the loneliness—what feelings of abandonment he must have experienced! We still had our parents and each other for comfort, but Roy was alone to deal with his grief and fears.

We had never seen Nelson again after his first day at school. All we had seen was a little wooden box being lowered into the ground. I remember trying to make sense of it all with the mind of a child.

I had walked into our mother's room shortly after the funeral service to find her with her arms wrapped around our nine-month-old brother, her face soaked with tears. "Mommy, why are you crying?" I asked.

"My child," she answered, "you have no idea." She was right. How could I understand, at the age of eleven, the excruciating grief she felt at having just lost her son and her fear that we could all be taken from her? Mom was all too familiar with the pain of losing a child. Fifteen years earlier, she had found Gerard, then three months old, lying still in his bed. Crib death was what the doctors had told her.

Nelson's life, although short, touched us all in many ways. The siblings not old enough to remember for themselves have through our stories come to know and love that little boy with the curly brown hair and the twinkle in his eyes. He taught us all in six short years how we should live. Sundays will always be a reminder to us of the special little boy who was taken to heaven on his special day.

After being crippled by polio, Roy was never able to run again, something most of us take for granted. He hopes to find himself running through fields someday with Nelson at his side.

Mom waited fifty years before being reunited with her dear little boys; Dad would be there before her, awaiting her arrival.

CHAPTER THREE

Blessings along the Way

Dad, age 30

The sun was shining brightly that Saturday morning; according to the weatherman, this would last all weekend. I was now an adult living in the Northwest Territories with my husband and son. The past three years had proven to be quite an outdoor adventure. We were one of three families heading down the

Ingram Trail to a familiar campground. Our vehicles were piled high with coolers, camping gear, and noisy children.

Shortly after arriving at our campsite, I had an uneasy feeling about staying overnight, but not wanting to disappoint our son, I kept it to myself. It was not long after that my husband suggested we return home after supper. Our friends tried to talk us into staying, but I went along with his decision. As soon as we had finished eating, we dismantled our tent, repacked our gear, and headed home with our disappointed eight-year-old in the backseat.

About an hour and a half out of town, we had to stop the vehicle as a huge black bear sauntered across the road in front of us. In the three years that I had spent in the north, this was my first encounter with a bear. The superstition about a black cat crossing one's path came to mind, but I quickly dismissed it with the thought that it did not apply to bears. From the safety of our vehicle, we admired the animal before it disappeared into the forest, allowing us to continue on our journey.

When we pulled into the driveway, I could hear the sound of the telephone ringing from the kitchen window. I ran in, and just as I was about to pick up the receiver I felt an odd sensation come over me. My brother's voice was barely audible as he gave me the news that Dad had just passed away.

I wanted so badly to be at home with Mom and my siblings, but home was 3,000 miles away in a small town in northern New Brunswick, and I had missed the last plane out of the north that evening. I did not sleep much that night, wanting anxiously to find a flight that would get me home as soon as possible. The local airline office would not open until Sunday morning, so I would just have to be patient.

The next morning I woke early and walked to church, where I knew I would find some peace. I sat in my pew, prayed for Dad's soul, and asked God to comfort Mom and my siblings.

Dad had survived his first heart attack five years earlier, but this time it was not meant to be. They had just returned home from a fiftieth wedding anniversary celebration. Our parents had left the church, briefly stopped at the reception hall to wish the couple well, and then returned home, where Dad had collapsed.

After I got home from church that morning, the airline office was open, and I was able to arrange a flight to Montreal, with a stopover in Winnipeg. The flight was scheduled to arrive in Montreal around midnight. This meant that I would have to wait until Monday morning to fly into my home province. All I wanted to do was get on that plane—I would worry about accommodations later. There was always the option of spending the night in the airport, although that thought frightened me. It was the first time that I had felt so isolated living in the north. I so desperately wanted to be home and felt so very alone in my grief.

Sunday afternoon I was able to board the plane that would take me to my family. When we touched down in Winnipeg, I knew the wait would be several hours. I walked to my gate and found an empty seat in the lounge, where I sat in a daze, staring off into the crowd. My eyes were soon drawn to an older woman sitting about six seats away from me. She looked remotely familiar. I kept looking at her and thinking, *why do I know her*? She vaguely resembled the picture that Mom kept on her dresser of her dear friend Dorothy. It was her graduation picture from nursing school. Dorothy had moved to Montreal when she was in her twenties, and although she and Mom had kept in touch, we had not seen her in years.

In fact, I had been seven years old the last time I saw her. I eventually did the math and realized that twenty-seven years had passed.

Could this be the dear, sweet woman who had taken the time each year when we were children to send us individual Christmas cards? Waiting for the mail was one of the highlights of our Christmas season, and the Christmas cards added to the magic with all those bright colours and glistening snow scenes! Pictures of Santa with his beautiful red suit and his shiny reindeer remain one of my fondest memories today. One by one, we would find special places on the tree for our cards and watch as our otherwise sparsely decorated Christmas tree took on new life.

I looked at the woman for a long time before mustering up the courage to approach her. "Are you Dorothy Imhoff?" I asked, not sure of her married name.

"Yes, I am," she replied. "But who are you?" she asked with a quizzical look on her face. I felt such relief at that moment and was so thankful that it was indeed my mother's friend. I knew that she would share my grief about my dad and that I would have someone to keep me company while I waited for the next flight.

"I'm Rosalie's daughter," I replied, "and I am on my way home because my father has passed away. I was not able to get a connecting flight to New Brunswick until tomorrow morning, and I have no place to stay," I quickly blurted out.

"Oh dear," she said, "I am so sorry to hear about your father. I was just here to attend my brother's funeral service. He spent years in the veterans' hospital, and I find comfort in knowing that his suffering is over. I am returning to my home in Montreal, and you can spend the night with me. I will be sure and get you to the airport on time for your flight."

I was a nursing student that year, and money was tight. The week before the phone call came I had received my credit card statement in the mail with a notice that my limit had been increased. It was just enough to cover the cost of my return ticket home. There were no banking machines in 1982, and the banks were not open on Sunday—not that it would have made a great difference. I felt sure that I was blessed in many ways during that trip.

When we boarded the plane for Montreal, Dorothy explained the circumstances to the flight attendants and asked if we could sit together. They were happy to make our trip as comfortable as possible.

Dorothy and I had a lot of catching up to do, so the time passed rather quickly. It did not seem long before the flight attendants made the announcement to fasten our seatbelts and prepare for landing.

We arrived in Montreal around midnight and took a short cab ride to their home, where her husband, James, greeted us. He was very happy to see his wife but surprised to see me. Dorothy introduced me and explained how we had met. James was saddened by the news about my father. After a short visit, I was tucked into bed, and as I lay my head on the pillow that night in the security and comfort of their home, I gave thanks, for I knew that Dorothy was an angel sent to help me.

The next morning I boarded the plane, and on my flight home, I sat there thinking about my father's life. I had always thought of him as such a strong man. He had had broad shoulders and large hands, and I always felt that he could accomplish anything. Dad had not been well the past five years; therefore, we should have been expecting something, but we were not prepared. You never think your parents are going to die until it happens. It all seemed so sudden.

From my earliest memories, he had had very little hair, and what he did have he kept smothered in Grecian formula. Dad was not short on imagination or on humour; it was his best—and sometimes most annoying—quality. He loved to tell the story about picking blueberries, when he was a young boy, to pay for the taxes on the family home. When the berries were ripe, one stick of Juicy Fruit gum was handed out to each of the children picking that day. This was done in the hope that it would decrease their appetites for the plump and delicious purple treats hanging from the bushes. The best part of the day for Dad was trying to entice his old aunt to the best picking spot and watching her squat over a bees' nest. Then the chase would be on with Dad at the lead and auntie in pursuit followed by some angry bees. How much more fun could a seven-year-old boy have? Four years later, his life would change drastically.

Dad's life was probably not much different from that of other children born in the early 1900s. He endured many hardships. When he was eleven years old, his mother died suddenly, leaving Grandpa to care for him and his three sisters, Gladys, Lise and Helen. A year later, Grandpa could no longer cope without his wife, and he sold the family home. Dad was sent to live on his uncle's farm, where he was treated poorly. Education was no longer an option, and he only ever learned to spell and recognize his own name. His sisters found jobs as housekeepers but had to move to other communities.

The following year, Dad hopped a freight train that would take him to the shores of Northern Quebec, where he spent the next sixteen years working in lumber camps. That is where he developed a love and knowledge of horses. He was a thirteen-year-old boy trying to survive in a man's world.

Dad never talked much about those days. I shudder to think what it must have been like for him.

As I look back on Dad's life, it is easy to understand some of his parenting methods. All he had was the knowledge he had learned as a child. His impressionable years were spent in the company of lumberjacks. He often spoke of his mother and his longing to see her. Dad had never forgotten Grandma's teachings about God and the importance of communicating with Him through prayer. For many years, his sisters kept him in their prayers and wished for his return home someday. It would take years, but their prayers would be answered.

When Dad was twenty-nine years old, he longed for his family, so he returned home with the hope that he could reunite with his sisters. His search brought him to Bathurst Mines, where he found his oldest sister, Gladys. She had married mom's brother, Herby, and that is when our mother met our father.

After a short courtship they were married, and they soon moved into their first home, which was the renovated henhouse on Grandpa's farm. How humbling for Mom, who had grown up in the farmhouse. My grandmother had been a talented tailor, and she had taught our mother how to be creative with a needle and thread. With Dad doing the heavy labour, she soon transformed the old henhouse into a little dollhouse. They could now begin their married life together.

Mom and Dad were very happy there, but after Marie was born, they needed a bigger place. As luck would have it, they were able to move into the now-vacant house behind the farm. Grandma was a rather frail woman who had spent many years in and out of the TB sanatorium, and Mom wanted to be close enough to help her. Dad would try his hand at farming, but he would soon return to the forest industry. It was all he knew how to do.

My thoughts soon transitioned back to the present as the plane made its final approach.

Mom was in great emotional pain when I arrived home, and we were all very concerned about her health. As she stood in the church a few days later by Dad's open casket, I saw her slip a note into his suit pocket. Then she quietly thanked him for their life together and the gift of their children. His shoes would be hard to fill, but she stepped up with grace and a strength that came from deep within as she assumed her place as the new head of our family.

We waited in anticipation for our brother to arrive from Alberta. Just minutes before the service began, the church doors opened. My heart broke as I watched Roy make his way down the aisle to our father's open casket. There would be no private time for him. He would have to say his goodbyes in front of all the family and friends who had gathered for the funeral Mass. The blessing was that he had been home a few months earlier, and he and Dad had enjoyed a wonderful visit.

A few days later, on my return flight home, I was wondering how Mom would cope. After forty-seven years of marriage, she would find herself alone for the first time. As I sat, I thought about friends I had known who had experienced the loss of a parent. I tended to shy away from grieving people because I was never sure what to do or say. I no longer do that, and I feel grateful if my experience can bring comfort to someone else.

The first Sunday after I arrived home, I went to Mass and was very surprised, but happy, to feel my father's presence in church. It was such a strong feeling that I could sense where he was standing on the altar. Some people believe that after a loved one dies God allows his or her soul to stay around for a short time to comfort the family. I believe it was my father's last gift to me. I was very anxious to return the following week, and again I could feel his presence, but that would be the last time. The next Sunday I ran to church, hoping that he would still be there, but he was gone, and although I felt sad, I could also find peace and comfort in knowing that he was now reunited with his mother, for whom he had so longed.

Twenty-seven years later, I am still wondering whether the bear encounter the night my father passed away was insignificant or an omen that darkness would soon descend upon our family. Could the grief and uncertainty eventually be replaced by a renewed sense of hope that comes with the dawning of a new day?

CHAPTER FOUR

A Woman of Courage

Mom in her late twenties.

The fall of 1986 was a sad time for our family. Mom had just celebrated her 71st birthday, and she had been diagnosed with cancer of the sinus cavity. Having lost our father a few years earlier, we were not prepared to give our mother up without a fight. She was referred to a cancer clinic in Montreal to see if anything could be done to prolong her life. The prognosis was good, and she was given two options. The first one was to do radical surgery, which included removing her hard palate, followed by reconstructive surgery, because the cancer had already infiltrated the sinus cavity. This would be followed by high doses of radiation. She chose the second option, which was to have the radiation only, and she asked to be referred to the Ottawa General Oncology unit. My sister Theresa and her husband, Gerry, were living nearby at the time, and this would mean that she would not be alone to face what would become a very long and painful ordeal. I had accompanied her to Montreal but would soon have to return to the north.

Before my mother could begin her radiation treatments, she had to have a mould made that was then used to make a mask of her face. The areas requiring radiation were marked and when all the technicalities were complete, it was time for her to begin her treatments. She would then have this tight mask placed over her face, and the edges fixed to the table to prevent any movement. This was the most difficult part for her. Although each treatment in itself was not long, the fact that she had to be restrained was very frightening and gave her the feeling that she was suffocating, but she continued with her treatments. I do not remember how many she had, but there were many. When her treatments were over, it meant that she could return to her home and resume her life. The doctors were all very encouraging; and with the treatments, they were hoping to extend her life by ten years.

There were several years when Mom managed quite well, and then her left eye started to protrude. The cause was pressure from a tumour at the back of her eye. It meant going back to Ottawa for more treatments to try to shrink the tumour; these caused her to lose sight in that eye. A short time later, there was a tumour decreasing her jaw mobility, so she had to have all her teeth removed, making it very difficult for her to eat. Throughout her many trips to Ottawa, she maintained a positive outlook and complained very little, but she spent many hours in prayer in the privacy of her room.

My sister Theresa and her husband were living in Alberta at the time. Therefore, in the fall of 1987, Gerry resigned from the police force, returned to New Brunswick, and moved in with our mother. Theresa would be there to help Mom, and Gerry would look after the upkeep of the house, allowing Mom to stay in her home as long as possible. Everyone was happy, especially our mother.

In the fall of 1992, I, along with my son, left the north to spend the year in New Brunswick. His father stayed behind and would be visiting during the Christmas holidays. Nelson would attend high school, and this gave me an opportunity to spend some time with my mother. I had left home at seventeen years of age, and I had some regrets about all the time I had spent away from my family. That year with Mom was a gift I will cherish forever.

We moved into our cottage, and each day while my son attended school, I would make my way to Mom's place, helping in any way that I could, yet still allowing her what little independence she had left.

I was able to help with meal preparation and spending time in my mother's company. She was still independent, but my sister was happier knowing that Mom would not be left on her own. Each day after lunch, Mom would retire to her room for a nap, and I would walk to the local nursing home and help to feed the residents who required some assistance. It was another enjoyable part of my day.

Each morning when Mom was feeling well, she would dress up as if she were going out and would appear in the kitchen, in good humour, smiling and happy to have another day. As I sat there one day watching her, the thought crossed my mind: *How does she do it?* By this time, it was very evident that she had a battle on her hands. She had already lost sight in her left eye. There was only a thin layer of skin covering the cheekbone. Her jaw was sunken from having had her teeth removed, and she was not able to open her mouth more than the width of a straw.

Our mother was a tall, elegant woman who prided herself in staying fit and looking her best. When she walked into a room, people noticed. She had that kind of energy, and she never complained. If she had any concern, it was about the possibility of transmitting her illness to her children.

One morning I watched her come out of her bedroom, all dolled up as usual. "How do you do it, Mom?" I asked. "With all that you have been through and all that is ahead of you, how do you do it?"

"I have a goal, my darling," was her reply.

"What is that?" I asked, having no idea what it could be.

"Well," she said, "I am trying to save ten thousand dollars so I can leave each of you one thousand, and I now have six thousand in my account."

Tears still well up in my eyes when I think back to that day. Mom had lived her whole life in poverty, had appreciated everything she had, was grateful for the children God had placed in her care, and she wanted to leave us all a little something. Ten thousand dollars is not a large sum of money by today's standards, but for our mother, who was saving this from her Old Age Security benefits, it would be an enormous achievement. She did accomplish her goal, with twelve dollars to spare.

At the end of June that year, Mom was still coping fairly well, and I had to return to my family. My sister would make alternate arrangements for her care.

During the next few years, she made many trips to Ottawa for more radiation and follow-up appointments. I was fortunate to be with her on several of these trips. When the doctors would say that they would see her in another three months, Mom would smile and say, "I guess they think I am going to make it to the next visit." That was all the reassurance she needed to keep moving forward.

On one of my visits home, I took Mom to Nova Scotia on the train to visit my brother Roy, Sherry and their son Matt, who had moved into their new home. Mom and I both loved the train, but it had become very difficult for her to eat in public. It took her a long time to swallow, and this made her very anxious, so instead of going to the dining car, we just sat in our seats and ordered from the snack cart.

People looked at her differently when they noticed her deteriorating outer appearance. *They have no idea who this wonderful person is,* I thought to myself. I sat there thinking of how often I had judged people by their outward appearances. I learned a valuable lesson that day. We are all so quick to judge what is on the outside instead of trying to discover the beauty that radiates from within.

The year before Mom died was a difficult time for her and everyone who loved her. Watching her deteriorate that way was extremely painful, especially for my sister and her husband, who became her primary caregivers.

During the month of September that year, our mother lost her memory. A tumour putting pressure on part of her brain was the likely cause. Theresa arranged caregivers to ensure that she was never left alone. That was the first time Mom had not acknowledged my birthday. I should have known that something was wrong. Since I lived so far away, my sister did not want to alarm me. Mom did regain her memory the last month of her life, for which we were very thankful.

Our mother had a great love of Christmas and all that went along with it. The week before she passed away, my sister Eddy and her two daughters, Stacy and Dawn, travelled from Ontario by train to spend some time with her. Although Mom's health was slowly deteriorating, we never really believed that she would leave us so soon. We just could not imagine life without her.

The week that Eddy and my nieces spent at the house was a blessing to all of them. Mom was able to spend time with her beautiful granddaughters. They put her in a wheelchair and walked through the mall. She enjoyed looking through the shop windows and listening to the sound of Christmas carols. Eddy danced her around the living room to some of her favourite music. Jackie had a family gathering, not knowing that Mom would be gone by Christmas. It was now mid-November, and Eddy and her girls would soon be heading home.

The evening before their departure, Mom was having breathing problems and they took her to the hospital. My sister was helping her to the car when she stopped to write in the freshly fallen snow with her cane the words *I love you*.

Eddy did not return to Ontario as planned. Our mother was admitted to the palliative care unit at our local hospital and after Mom was resting comfortably, my sisters settled into the lounge. During the night, Mom's condition worsened, and she asked the nurses to call her children, as she wanted them with her.

I received a phone call late Sunday evening, and I arranged to fly home on Monday morning. Mom's condition had improved a bit, so I was very anxious but hopeful that I could see her one more time.

I was not able to get a direct flight home, so it would be a long day that seemed even longer because of the urgency I felt. I prayed as I had never prayed before that Mom would still be alive when I got there. We sure can plead with God when we find ourselves in a crisis. I said decade after decade of the rosary for each of my siblings, who I knew were suffering like myself with the realization that Mom would soon be leaving us and we could not stop it.

On the last leg of my journey, I sat by a woman who asked me where I was going. Through tear-filled eyes, I told her, and I mentioned my fear that I would not arrive on time. She told me not to worry, that my mother would still be there when I got home. I hoped that she was right.

While my family was keeping vigil at our mother's bedside, Mom was asking for me, as I was the only one who had not yet arrived. I had to fly into the Moncton airport, which was a two-and-a-half-hour drive to my hometown. The plane landed at 10:00 p.m., and since I had not had any contact with the family for several hours, I was happy to see my brother Andrew and grateful to hear that Mom was waiting for me. My sisters kept reassuring her that I would be there shortly after midnight.

It was a long drive back, and when I arrived at the hospital, I ran up to my mother's room. My heart almost stopped when I saw family members standing in the hallway outside her door. I thought that I was too late. My sister Evelyn recognized the look of panic on my face and said, "She's waiting for you."

When I walked into the room, Mom made the sign that she loved me. "I love you too, Mom," I replied as I held her in my arms. Because of the many tumours inside her mouth,

Mom was no longer able to speak, but I was grateful that she was still alive and alert. She tried to talk to me, but the words would not come out. I often wondered what she was trying to say. I would find out years later when she came to my sister in a dream. Tina asked Mom what she had been trying to tell me that night in the hospital. "I wanted to wish her a happy birthday," she told her. She had not forgotten.

There was a full moon in the sky that night, and Mom brought it to my attention. I have always enjoyed watching the moon. When I do, I think back to that night in the hospital and how Mom, in her weakened state, was still able to appreciate the beauty of the universe. I spent most of that night at her bedside. The nursing staff administered medication while my sister and I provided her nursing care.

On Tuesday morning, Mom slipped into a coma. We took turns sitting at her bedside, talking to her and reciting her beloved rosary. I did not want to leave her bedside because I wanted to be there until the end, but it was not meant to be. As I sat by her bed, I soon came to the realization that I had to get out of my nurse's role and let the nurses care for her physical needs. Then I could allow myself to grieve with my siblings.

I had not been able to sleep or choke down much food for two days, so on Wednesday morning our brothers suggested that I and a few of my sisters should go to our mother's house and get some sleep. I never questioned their suggestion, and they promised to call if things changed.

Mom had regained consciousness a short time before I went to her bedside to say goodbye. She looked at me for what would be the last time, and a tear in her beautiful blue eye glistened like a star. It reminded me of the star in the east that led the way to the stable where Jesus was born. I gently wiped the tear from her cheek, and knowing it was her final blessing, I used it to place a cross on my forehead. One by one, my siblings followed, and when each of us had received a blessing from our mother's tears, they stopped falling.

I quietly followed my sisters out of the hospital, and when we arrived at Mom's house, I immediately went to her room and lay on the bed. I sobbed for a long time. Then the most amazing thing happened! My eyes were closed yet I could see fireworks going off in the sky. I opened and closed my eyes several times to see if the picture would disappear, but each time I closed my eyes it was still there. It was like the July 1 celebrations. While this was happening, the telephone rang, and it was my brother telling us that we should go back to the hospital, but I declined. I had wanted to be with Mom until the end, and I still wonder today why I did not go back. After the second call a short time later, I agreed to return, but I knew in my heart that she would not be there.

Our sister Tina had a similar experience. She had walked out of the hospital and was standing beside a tall woman who was trying to engage her in conversation. There was also a van circling the parking lot, which she found very annoying. She just wanted some quiet time, and since she was not going to get it outside, she decided to return to Mom's room. She had been about to leave, when the woman told her to look up. It was an overcast day, but when Tina looked up, the clouds had parted to expose the most magnificent red sky she had ever seen. Shortly after that, she returned to our mother's room and found her lying peacefully in her bed.

When my brother-in-law Gerry drove us back to the hospital, he drew our attention to a magnificent rainbow arched over the hospital. The signs were everywhere.

When we arrived, our siblings met us and told us that Mom had just passed away. Jackie was holding her and quietly singing a French song, "Hold a Child in Your Arms."

In my twenty years of nursing, I had observed people dying and the unpleasant process some patients experience as the body systems shut down. Our mother did not exhibit any of those signs.

She looked like a porcelain doll lying in her bed. Her body remained warm, and her skin had a soft pink glow until she took her last breath.

The cancer that had once ravaged her face was barely visible. "She left this world with the faith, courage, and grace with which she lived." These words were taken from a poem written by her grandson Eric.

As I was leaving the house the next morning on my way to the funeral home to finalize arrangements, I could hear the dog whimpering in the backyard. She obviously missed seeing Mom every morning and could sense that something was wrong. I approached her and said, "You know that she is gone, don't you, Lady?" and then the whimpering stopped.

My son arrived from the north and he, along with several of his cousins, was both proud and honoured to be a part of his grandmother's service as he helped carry her body to its final resting place.

Family and friends gathered to bid farewell to this lovely lady, the woman we were privileged to call our mother. Our brother led us in prayer as we gathered at the graveside that cold November morning. The sun was shining brightly, and it reflected the blue of the coffin back to the sky as it was being lowered into the ground. There was no way of knowing where the sky ended and the earth began. The circle had been completed.

CHAPTER FIVE

A Winter Rose

It was the day after Mom's funeral, and my brother Edward and I were attending the regular Sunday service. I sat in my pew admiring the last bouquet of long-stemmed red roses my siblings and I had purchased for her. The attendants had placed them before the statue of Mary after the funeral Mass. My brother felt that the bouquet should be brought to our mother's grave. After the service, we gathered the roses and walked to the graveyard situated at the back of the church. The temperature had dropped the night before, and the ground was now frozen. We quickly placed some roses on the fresh grave; others we propped up against the tombstone, and the remainder we placed inside the already-frozen wreaths before returning home.

Theresa and I would spend part of the next week going through Mom's personal effects. I tried to do some Christmas baking, but it did not taste like Mom's. One day my sister Marie and I decided to trace our mother's steps back to where she had grown up and began her life with Dad. Our first stop was to visit our cousin Freddy, who had loved our mother like his own. He had spent many summers with us as a child, and Mom had been a positive influence in his life.

When we arrived at his home, his wife, Marjorie, greeted us. I told her that Theresa had sent Freddy a keepsake from

Mom's bedroom. She called him in from another room. He was very touched to receive the beautiful ceramic statue of the Virgin Mary. The fact that it had belonged to his Aunt Rose made it very special, and having it delivered to him on his birthday was truly a blessing. We had had no idea that it was his birthday. This was one of life's special moments.

Next, we headed up to see our cousin Marie, who had offered to take me to the airport that Friday morning. We sat and enjoyed a soothing cup of tea before heading back to my sister's place.

The next day, Theresa and I drove to town and decided to have lunch at our mother's favourite restaurant. On our return trip, Theresa asked if I would stop at the post office, which was situated across the road from our church. When she returned to the vehicle, I asked did she mind if I went back to the graveside, since I would be flying home the next morning. We had gotten a snowstorm two days earlier, so the ground was covered in a white blanket, making walking very difficult. Theresa chose to wait in the vehicle.

I walked the short distance to my parents' grave, and as I stood there, looking around at the frozen and wilted flower arrangements, my eyes were drawn to the roses that my brother and I had placed there five days earlier. They were still as beautiful as the day we had placed them. It was difficult to understand how the roses could have weathered the storm. These same roses had been inside the funeral parlour for three days, then in the church for one day, and then out in the wind, cold, and drifting snow for five more days. They looked as if they had just come from the florist. I carefully picked up a rose from the snow and walked to the vehicle to show Theresa, who was also bewildered. I carefully carried the rose back to her home and two days later it was in full bloom. We will never forget our gentle mother, and we are reminded of her each time we see a rose. Perhaps she was trying to tell us that she had gone to a place where roses never die.

My niece Dawn Johnson wrote this poem as she sat quietly by her grandmother's bed the day before she passed away. She simply wrote what she observed.

A Christian Woman

A sweet Christian woman
Lying in a bed
So many children lay their loving touch
Upon her head
As time grows near
She awakes to shed a tear
A promise of love and faith
Will hold the family near
The pain has held her life too long
Yet her praises to God are still sweet songs
Therefore, God has come to her bedside
To take her soft and weakened hand
Now, He will help
The sweet Christian woman stand
She will walk with Him
Another mile
But not as the old lady she was,
As the young, innocent child
That she again has become
God smiles upon her
Happy to gain back another one of His children
Rosalie skips alongside the Lord
Stops and turns once more to say goodbye

To those behind and to the happiness she knows they will find

They approach the gate

And He turns to her and says,

"My child, life has been hard, but now this is your fate."

CHAPTER SIX

My Christmas Present

I was sitting in the airport lounge visiting with my cousin Marie, thankful that she had offered to drive me there. Everyone else had gone back to resume their lives, and now it was time for me to return to my family. I was happy that I had stayed an extra week to help my sister dispose of Mom's personal effects. The house would have seemed too empty if we had all left at the same time. My siblings were sad that I would be travelling back to the north by myself, but I had reassured them that I would not be alone. I had the memories of our dear mother to keep me company. She had had a ten-year battle with cancer, and although we were happy that her suffering was finally over, we would all miss her terribly.

This woman had raised twelve children. She was a woman of faith with a kind heart and a wonderful way of making us all feel special. My siblings and I were all adults now, but to our mother we had always been her little babies. We were seven girls and five boys, and we ranged in age from our eldest sister at fifty-four to our youngest brother, who was now thirty-seven. Three of us lived away from home, but our youngest sister and her family had moved in with our mother shortly after her diagnosis.

Christmas would never be the same without Mom. How I had always loved the walk to the post office in the freezing cold to claim my parcel. However, there would be no hand-stitched socks this year for my son and his dad and no little something for me.

My sister Theresa had always helped with Mom's Christmas shopping. This time, in early November, she had asked our mom what she wanted to buy us. Mom had replied, "This year, my darling, I will give them each a twenty-dollar bill." Mom had never given us money as gifts; it was a sure sign that her health was failing.

My cousin and I were still chatting in the airport lounge when two staff members from the security counter approached us and asked if I was taking the next flight. When I answered that I was, they said that I should proceed through security. I looked around the airport and saw many people milling about, and I wondered, *Why me*? I have often thought about why I was centered out that day. Nonetheless, I said my goodbyes to my cousin and headed to the counter.

While they were checking my carry-on, I looked up and saw, sitting all by herself, a tall grey-haired woman wearing a purple trench coat similar to the one Mom wore. She reminded me so much of my mother that I could feel sadness sweep over me. She smiled and turned her head. When the security staff returned my luggage, I hesitated for a moment, but I felt drawn to this woman, so I walked over and took the seat next to her. She asked if I could speak French, and when I said yes, she said that I had smiled at her from the security desk and that it had warmed her heart. I had no recollection of smiling but was happy that I had.

I sat in my seat weeping, and she did not ask why. Instead, she proceeded to tell me about the crumpled five-dollar bill she had found on the floor, which belonged to a young fellow, and she pointed in his direction. She had given him back his money, and she said that he would not get too far with five dollars and laughed.

Her boarding pass was sitting on her lap, and I asked her destination. "Oh," she said, "I am on my way to Edmonton, with a stop in Montreal." When I told her that I too was going to Edmonton, en route to Yellowknife, she said, "We are going to be friends," and patted my hand.

A short time later they called our flight, and while I was gathering my bags, she stood there waiting for me. When we entered the plane, I noticed the young man who had lost the five-dollar bill about to sit in the seat next to my new friend. I asked him if he could change seats with me. Without saying a word, he gathered his belongings and quickly moved to my assigned seat at the back of the plane.

As soon as the plane had reached cruising altitude, my travelling companion said that she needed to use the washroom. We were flying in a small plane in which I had travelled many times before, so I suggested that she remove her coat because the washroom was tiny. She also handed me her purse to hold. I thought it very odd that she would trust her purse to a total stranger.

En route to Montreal, the flight attendant came by and asked if we wanted anything to drink. Before my friend could answer, I knew instinctively that she would ask for orange juice. While we were enjoying our drinks, she asked me if I was going on a vacation, to which I answered that I was returning to my home. She then asked if I was visiting my parents. When I told her that I had been home to see my sick mother and that she had passed away, I started to cry. She said, "Do not worry, my darling. It will be okay." My mother often used the words *my darling* when speaking to her children. How comforting to hear them so soon after she had gone! The woman never questioned me after that, but she told me that her children had been concerned for her safety and had cautioned her to be very careful of strangers. Then she said, "But it feels just like having my daughter next to me."

When she told me that she had raised twelve children, seven girls and five boys, and that three of her children lived away from home, my curiosity was sparked. She then proceeded to tell me that her eldest was a girl of fifty-four and her youngest was a boy of thirty-seven. "All my children are good to me," she said, "but I live with my youngest daughter." She then dozed off. My mind was racing—there were so many similarities!

Just before she woke up, the flight attendant came by a second time and asked if I wanted a beverage. I ordered tea for both of us, and once again, I knew that she took it with milk, no sugar. As she sipped her cup of tea, she commented that it was just the way she liked it. "When we arrive in Montreal, I want to buy your lunch," she said.

We spoke about her interests, such as card parties, Bingo, and dances at the Legion—the same things my mother enjoyed. How could this be? How could these women have lived such similar lives? The more we talked, the more I was drawn to her. It felt as if I knew her and she knew me. It all seemed so natural and comfortable.

She then proceeded to tell me that she was going to Edmonton to surprise her son, whom she had not seen since his father had died ten years before on November 20. November 20 was same date that my mother had passed away. The more she spoke, the more excited and curious I became. I asked if I could see her ticket. When she handed it to me, I saw that she was booked on a different plane to Edmonton, leaving two hours later. We were both disappointed that we would not be on the same flight, so I told her that I would try to get her ticket changed when we arrived at the airport. She did not think it possible, because she had purchased her ticket months earlier and had been given a special rate. I reassured her that it was still worth trying. I could not imagine leaving her so soon.

When our plane pulled up to the gate, a man in an Air Canada uniform, pushing a wheelchair, met us. The lady's family had made arrangements for the wheelchair because she had difficulty walking long distances. I offered to push the chair, but the man insisted on helping us. When we arrived inside the terminal, I explained our circumstances and asked him if my friend's ticket could be changed to coincide with my departing flight. I then handed him both tickets, and he disappeared behind the ticket counter. What seemed like a short time later, he returned with both tickets and indicated that we would be flying out at the same time and that she would be sitting next to me. I was both relieved and happy, knowing that I would have a few more hours to spend with her. I offered to pay the difference for changing her ticket, but the gentleman from Air Canada said, "Non, madame, it would cost too much money, and we have (referring to the airline) enough money anyway." We were both so grateful for his kindness. We were then given the directions to the restaurant and told how to find the gate for the next leg of our journey. After hugs and kisses, he left us on our own.

We made our way to the restaurant on the second floor, and when my new friend was sitting comfortably, she handed me thirty dollars and said, "Would you go and buy us some lunch?" It was cafeteria style, so I walked up to the counter and ordered what I thought she would like. While we were enjoying our meal, I tried to tell her about the similarities—and they were many—between herself and my now-deceased mother, but she looked at me with a look that said, "Don't go there." I did not pursue it any further. I was not sure what was happening, but being in her company brought me a great sense of comfort.

We still had some time after lunch, so I decided to make a stop at the beauty salon for a haircut. I had left home rather quickly and was badly in need of one. It would also help pass the time. When I walked into the salon, I positioned the wheelchair next to the chair in which I would be sitting so we could still chat. The hair stylist asked me to follow her to the sink, which was situated to the right of the salon behind a partition wall.

When she had finished shampooing my hair, I sat up, and in the mirror, I saw a reflection of my mother sitting in the wheelchair. Her face no longer bore the signs of the cancer. I shook my head in disbelief, and when I turned back, the image was gone. Had my mind been opened to a place where angels soar? Confused by what had just taken place, I returned to the chair with mixed feelings of joy and sorrow and found my friend sitting quietly waiting for me. Who would ever believe this story? I could barely make sense of it myself. Just as I was about to sit, she said, "You will look good for your husband and son." I could not remember telling her that I had a son.

She insisted on paying for my haircut. Mom and I had made many trips to Ottawa when she was undergoing radiation treatments. I would sometimes fly from the north and meet her; occasionally I would accompany her from her home. She would always want to pay for the expenses, but I would never allow her. She was on a limited income, and I felt that it was time to give back. There was something inside telling me that I needed to accept *this* lady's generosity.

It was soon time to report to the gate for our next flight. Before boarding the plane, I made a quick call for her to her daughter-in-law, who knew about the surprise visit. I explained who I was and told her that she would be arriving two hours earlier than originally planned. There was not one empty seat on the flight as we departed from Montreal. After a short stop in Toronto, we were en route to Edmonton.

I had always had a fear of flying, but on that day, my fear disappeared, never to return. I remember thinking that even if the plane did somersaults I would not be afraid.

A short time into the flight, my travelling companion fell asleep. A woman sitting on my right said, "You seem so close," with a look of envy on her face. I then told her that I had just met this lady that morning and that there were many similarities between her and the mother I had recently lost. "Write the story down," she said. "It needs to be told."

After my companion woke from her nap, she needed help with several things. They were simple things, from opening a bag of peanuts to loosening her bootlaces. Everything I did was effortless, and yet she was so grateful. There was a moment when I noticed tears in her eyes and asked if she was feeling unwell. "You have no idea," she replied, "of the joy that is in my heart to have you here with me."

I had introduced myself to her earlier that morning, but I did not grasp her name until near the end of the day when I asked her for the third time. "My name is Angelina," she replied.

We were about to start our descent into Edmonton. Angelina looked at me with tear-filled eyes, held my hand, and said, "My darling, I am so proud of you. You have done so much for me, I cannot tell you." She then handed me a crumpled twenty-dollar bill she had removed from her purse and said, "This is your Christmas present. Put it in a safe place."

I thanked her and sat there in disbelief, thinking to myself, *How can this be happening?* I then placed the gift that Angelina had given me in my pocket and remained speechless until the plane was on the ground.

When we walked into the airport, there was a lone wheelchair, and I helped Angelina into it. Then we headed to the baggage department. Shortly afterwards we were greeted by her son and daughter-in-law. Her son was so surprised and happy to see his mother! It had been too long since their last visit. After we were introduced, Angelina said that she would like a picture of us. I crouched down beside the wheelchair, and just before her daughter-in-law snapped the picture, Angelina reached up, and in a loving gesture that was so familiar to me, she cupped my face with her hand, just as Mom always had. It was difficult to say goodbye to this lovely lady I had only known for twelve hours, and yet there was something so special about our encounter that it seemed to transcend to the supernatural.

Shortly after, I boarded the next flight on the last leg of my journey. I fell fast asleep, emotionally exhausted, and woke as the plane was landing in Yellowknife.

When I arrived home, I removed the crumpled twenty-dollar bill from my pocket and saw, worn but still visible, the stamp from the Royal Bank. This was the place where Mom had always done her banking. The first two letters signifying the month of November were still legible, but the date was missing. Did the number 20 on the bill represent the date of her passing?

Mom had spoken to all my siblings before she died. By the time I had arrived at the hospital she had lost her ability to speak. Oh, she had tried, but the words would not come. I had felt heartbroken—but now I was the only one who had received my Christmas present that year and a total stranger had delivered it to me. Or was she?

CHAPTER SEVEN

A Special Rainbow

My grief was still raw when I returned home from Mom's funeral. I was happy to get back to work. My love of nursing and the responsibility of caring for my patients provided me with a purpose as I tried to mend my broken heart. Christmas was fast approaching, and although I went through the motions of shopping and baking, I was not looking forward to the day. Without Mom, the special holidays would never be the same. Change is often difficult to accept when you are not part of the decision-making.

The overwhelming sadness I felt when I would encounter an elderly woman or a mother and daughter was difficult to overcome. A sweet woman who attended our church had lost her husband the same week that my mother had passed away, so I would often find myself at her door. Thankfully I was always welcomed, and over a cup of tea we would both sit and cry. We understood each other's need to grieve, and I always felt better when I left her home. Because I lived so far from my family I was happy to have a safe place to visit when I was feeling sad. The first two months were especially difficult, so I thought that I should apply to my own situation a line that I had once read in a poem: "Bury your sorrows in doing good." I decided to spend more of my free time volunteering.

Back at home in early December, I had received a wonderful gift in the mail from my sister Marie. The picture had hung in our mother's bedroom for many years. It dated back to the early 1800s, and the image is of a mother sitting and a child kneeling in prayer. The picture that had been passed down by three generations of grandmothers. My sister thought that it should remain in our family and that Mom would want me to have it. I was grateful for her generosity. Since she was the eldest, it should rightfully have gone to her. I knew that my family were worried about me and wondered how I was handling our loss. They had thought that a parcel from home might help to cheer me up. I had always admired my mother's picture, but what my sister did not know was that years earlier I had purchased a similar one in an antique store.

One week before the parcel arrived, my son had announced that he would soon be moving out of our home and sharing an apartment with friends. He asked if he could take a few items with him. One of those items was the antique picture that was hanging on my bedroom wall. I had been reluctant to part with the picture, but I told him that he could have it. I was pleased, yet surprised that he had even noticed the picture—and more amazed that he would want it. Each day when I walked past the bare wall, I wondered how I could ever find a replacement. Now I could replace it with my mother's picture. It still hangs on my bedroom wall today. I feel a special connection to the ancestral women I have never met who were also drawn to this beautiful picture depicting a mother teaching her child how to pray. I have memories of my mother in that role.

I tried to carry on with my life, but I still missed my mother every day. Often I would pick up the telephone to call her and then realize she was gone. Volunteering was keeping me busy, and I enjoyed the time I could spend with the seniors. That is how I met Rose Fleming. She was in her early seventies and a resident at the local nursing home. The home had provided a refuge from the life of poverty and abuse she had endured for many years. Her scars, both physical and emotional, had left her with a broken spirit. Rose had not experienced much joy in her life, but through it all, as a child of God, she had remained a woman of faith.

It was hard to believe that nearly a year had gone by and November 20 was fast approaching. I wondered what I could do to celebrate the anniversary of Mom's life. I decided that it would be nice to take my friend Rose out for lunch. I loved the fact that she and Mom shared the same name, and I knew that Mom would have been pleased.

When I woke up that morning, I hoped that the sun would be shining, but there was an overcast sky. It was a "blah" day, much like the mood I was experiencing. I spent the morning reflecting on the last year of Mom's life, remembering the wonderful moments we had shared, her great sense of humour, and the Christmas she had spent with me in the north. I remembered the visits back home, the many telephone conversations that had made me feel like I was right there, and those wonderful memories leading up to the last four days of her life. I had been anxious and dreading this day. I knew in my heart that it was time for me to let go of the past year and move forward.

I arrived at the nursing home at around 11:30. Rose was sitting in her wheelchair, happily waiting for me and looking forward to an outing. I was grateful that she was able to spend part of this day with me. After greeting her, and with a bit of manoeuvring, I helped Rose into the vehicle, and once the wheelchair was placed in the trunk, we were on our way.

I had chosen a restaurant in the old part of town because I knew that Rose would enjoy both the cuisine and the drive.

A short time later, I was helping her out of the car and into the restaurant. I selected a table in front of the window and then positioned the chair so that Rose could be facing into the restaurant. I knew that she would enjoy watching the people moving about. I sat in my seat facing the window, still hoping that the sun would break through the dull sky. When the waiter came over, we placed our orders and sat there chatting as we waited patiently for our food to arrive.

I was thinking back to that day that had been just a year earlier and yet seemed like a lifetime away. Then I looked into the sky, and my heart burst with joy as I watched a beautiful rainbow unfold before my eyes. I sat in awe of its magical beauty and could feel its energy as it surrounded us. This was a special rainbow. Not only did it appear in late November, when winter in the north can arrive as early as October, but it also appeared exactly one year after the rainbow marking Mom's departure from this world. There was no sign of rain, and the sun never appeared that day, just the rainbow in all its magnificence. I was humbled to think of all the wonders and mysteries of the universe and its Creator.

Rose and I finished our meals, and as we made our way back to the nursing home, a sense of peace swept over me. With it came the knowledge that it was now time to allow my mother the freedom to continue on her journey. I am certain that our souls will reconnect when my allotted time in this world is over. With a thankful heart, I look to the future.

CHAPTER EIGHT

The Power of Love

This is a story that my niece Sidney shared with me several years after my mother's death.

The air was rather crisp that November morning in 1999, as Sidney walked to work. Her thoughts drifted back to her grandmother as she made a mental note to take her winter coat out of storage. She remembered the day her brother had purchased it for her at the second-hand store. It was brown, with gold patches and shiny buttons, and it was a little big for her tiny frame. Each time Sidney wore the coat someone would remind her how terrible it looked. It was warm and cozy, and she rather fancied that old coat.

Three years earlier, before her grandmother's death, Sidney had been struggling with direction for her life. Now she was finally doing what she loved, and she knew that her grandmother would be proud. It had been a long journey. She reflected back to when she had been thinking of becoming a nurse.

After high school, she had hoped to enter the nursing program. However, her transcripts had been lost and never reached the university. During the last week of registration, she had been able to enrol in the science program, and she had hoped that by the following year she would be able to enter the nursing program. After the first year was over, Sidney was no longer sure that she wanted to pursue a career in nursing. She continued with the science program but dropped out after completing her third year. She felt confused and did not know what direction she should take. There was no point in adding an extra financial burden for her parents. She decided to move to the city and share an apartment with a girlfriend. During that time, her grandmother's health was declining.

Sidney remembered wearing the old coat the day she was called to the hospital in early November. As she entered the room, she recognized her grandmother's weakened voice. "I love your coat," she said.

Sidney walked over to the bedside and whispered, "I love you, *Mémère*." She instantly felt better. All she had needed was her grandmother's approval.

"Are you happy?" she asked.

Sidney was not prepared for that question. How could she tell her dying grandmother that she was struggling with so many things? How typical of her grandmother to be concerned about everyone but herself! "I had to lie," she told me. "I just could not tell her the truth." But deep in her heart she knew that her grandmother could sense her unhappiness. They had a very close relationship, and Sidney knew that she would soon be losing her.

Then, on November 27, "I should be happy about my birthday," she told me, but she was not. In fact, she was feeling very sad that day. She had buried her dear grandmother a week earlier. How could she be happy? She missed her terribly. She was the only grandmother Sidney had ever known, the grandmother who always blew her kisses as she was leaving her house, the grandmother she could always count on for advice and support, and the person she knew loved her unconditionally.

Sidney wandered around the streets that dreary day and felt shame. She disliked the thought that her grandmother would be disappointed with the shape her life was taking. She felt lost and could not seem to find her way. *Where do I go from here?* she wondered. Her job in a small shop was barely covering the bills, not to mention all the student loans.

She walked around for several hours, until she found herself in a ballpark. She noticed a bench in the distance and, as she walked over to it, felt even more sadness. She looked around at the brown grass, once green and filled with the sound of happy feet, but today everything around her was bleak and lifeless. *Not a speck of colour to be seen*, she thought as she plunked herself on the bench. A row of naked maple trees stood at her back.

Sidney had just turned twenty-two, yet she felt very old that day. She was sitting there sniffling, when an elderly woman approached her and asked if she could sit beside her. Sidney noticed that the woman's face was somewhat distorted. It reminded her of the ravaging effects the cancer had had on her grandmother's face.

"Why are you crying, dear?" the elderly woman asked.

Sidney told the woman that she had recently lost her grandmother and that she missed her terribly. "She offered me a candy, and I found her presence to be somewhat calming," she later told me.

"Your grandmother would want you to be happy," the woman said.

A short time later, when she was a bit more composed, Sidney stood up to leave. "Take care, dear," the woman, told her as she walked away.

A few nights later, Sidney had a dream. She was in a beautiful park that was ablaze with colours. There were many flowers and shrubs of different shapes and sizes. "It was so peaceful, and I was so happy there," she said. "I walked around, taking in the beauty of the bright pinks, yellows, and reds against the green foliage. It was like finding myself in the centre of a huge bouquet. I stopped for a moment to absorb the wonderful, intoxicating fragrances. I then noticed a park bench in the distance, and as I got closer, I could see that my grandmother was sitting on the bench. I was so happy to see her.

"She looked lovely in her pink and blue floral dress with the white collar and cuffs. It was her favourite—the reason why her children had chosen the outfit for her burial. Her beautiful silver hair was combed neatly. It was all very peaceful in the garden, and Grandma looked beautiful. The signs of her cancer were no longer visible."

Sidney approached the bench and sat beside her. There were no words exchanged between them, until Sidney noticed the large book that was sitting on her grandmother's lap. The word *energy* was written across the cover in bold letters. There was light shining through each letter, illuminating the word. *Energy, energy*, she repeated to herself and wondered about its significance.

It was all very quiet and calm in the park, and the air was still. Sidney kept looking at the book on her grandmother's lap. She finally asked, "*Mémère*, what does that mean?" as she pointed to the word.

Her grandmother turned to her and said, "Sidney, my darling, energy is the key to your happiness."

"What happened next?" I asked her.

Sidney said, "She then placed her arms around me and held me for a long time. She never spoke another word, but she emitted so much love that I was filled with such a wonderful sense of peace, like nothing I had ever experienced before."

Sidney confided that when she'd awakened the next morning she'd been happy for the first time in years and knew that she would be okay. Her dream was still vivid and she wanted to share it with someone, so she woke her roommate, who was also touched by her story.

After lunch, the girls decided to take a stroll around town. They walked down the street and wandered around until they came upon a shop called Little Mysteries. The name was intriguing, so they decided to stop and browse a bit. As they entered the shop, her girlfriend Mary stopped to examine the notices and flyers posted on the wall at the entrance. Sidney wandered around, and then she heard her girlfriend's voice. "Oh my God, Sidney," she said, "come and see this!"

Sidney quickly walked back to join her friend. "What's wrong?" The words were no sooner off her lips when she noticed a flyer in Mary's outstretched hand. It had the word *energy* written across the top in bold letters.

"This is like your dream!"

It was an advertisement for a new school that had recently opened on the street where they lived, a school of natural health and well-being. "I have to go there," Sidney told her friend with a sense of urgency in her voice. "I need to see that place."

Sidney's spirit soared as she left the little shop, the flyer tucked away in her pocket. She wondered where this would lead her.

The next morning, she made her way to the school and discovered that they were offering several programs. When she looked at the massage therapy program, she knew in her heart that it was what she wanted to do. Unfortunately, the program was full, so she decided to enrol in the reflexology program. The following year, she was certain that she wanted to pursue a career in massage therapy, and she registered in the program. After the second semester of the two-year program, the school closed, leaving many students scrambling to find placements. A branch of the Northumberland Massage Therapy School in Halifax, Nova Scotia, opened, and Sidney was able to join in with the first-year group.

In 1999, three years after her grandmother had passed away, Sidney graduated as a registered massage therapist. "It has been life-changing," she told me. She loves her career and is very thankful for the guidance that came to her in her dream. Each year on her birthday, she takes out the last birthday card she received from her grandmother and displays it proudly with the others. When family members visit Sidney, she remembers to blow them a kiss as they are leaving her home. It was something her beloved Memere had always done. Her years with her grandmother were too few, but the memories will last a lifetime.

CHAPTER NINE

The Gift

Propped up in his hospital bed, he looked like an old man, with his long grey hair and beard to match. His blue eyes were the colour of the sky on a clear day. Pierre was his name, and he had spent the best years of his life working underground. He was now bedridden, and for the past two years of his five-year confinement, he had been dependent on oxygen for his very existence.

My volunteer services as a barber had brought me to their home, where his wife, Teresa, greeted me. She was a tall, slender woman who appeared timid and unsure about allowing a stranger to enter her world. I noticed a stale smell in the air as I followed Teresa into her husband's room, located off the main entrance. The hospital bed occupied most of the space, which was small and sparsely furnished. The radio on the nightstand beside his bed was silent. There was a curtain over the only window in the room, which gave it a sombre feel.

The home-care nurse who had arranged my visit said that Pierre was long overdue for a haircut and she hoped that I could do something with his unruly beard. He was about to celebrate his sixty-ninth birthday, and Teresa wanted him to look his very best.

After the haircut and beard trim, challenging as it was in such a confined area, I offered to return on a weekly basis to assist with Pierre's grooming. Teresa seemed grateful for the help and graciously accepted.

Pierre had met Teresa in Mexico City, on one of his work adventures, and had won over her heart. Much to the sorrow and disapproval of her parents, she had headed to northern Canada with her husband, twenty-five years her senior, to begin her new life as the wife of a gold miner.

She had been a mere child when she left the familiarity of her home to travel to a foreign land, speaking very little English. Her only contact with her family was by mail or the occasional phone call when money permitted. Pierre's poor health had forced him into early retirement and put a huge strain on their limited income.

Teresa's social life for the past few years had consisted of visits from the community nurses, quick trips to the grocery store, and church services on Sundays, when a friend was available to sit with Pierre. The endless chatter of her two budgie birds brought a smile to her often-sad face. She soon welcomed me into her circle.

When Pierre and I discovered that we had both grown up in northern New Brunswick, of French parents, we had lots to talk about and stories to tell. . . . One day, while I was washing his hair and comparing our Roman Catholic upbringings, Teresa popped her head into the room and said, "Do not bother talking to Pierre about religion; he is an atheist, you know," and she smiled. I sensed feelings of unworthiness within Pierre when I spoke with him, and I was uncertain where those feelings came from. We finished our conversation, and after my usual cup of tea, I left, with plans to return the following Tuesday.

Each week I tried to share my time equally between them, and our friendship grew. Teresa confided to me that Pierre had been a heavy drinker and that life had not always been easy for her.

On one of my visits, she announced that Pierre's daughter from his first marriage was coming to visit, from Nova Scotia. Teresa did not have any children of her own, and she seemed quite pleased about the visit. It had been years since Pierre had seen his daughter, and their relationship had been somewhat strained due to the divorce.

The following Saturday night, I went to bed and dreamed that I had gone to visit Pierre. I remember thinking how nice it was that his daughter would see him before he died. We chatted as usual, and when it was time to leave, in an affectionate, fatherly gesture, Pierre reached up with the fingers of his right hand and tickled the tip of my nose.

Waking up the following morning, I was amazed at the clarity of my dream. How vivid it was in my mind! I was thinking that, since it was Father's Day, I should visit Pierre and take him a gift. Perhaps I could go after I attended our church service.

It was a short walk to the little country church. When I arrived, I took my usual seat near the front and was still preoccupied with my dream when the Mass began. I was trying to decide what I could buy Pierre on a Sunday, knowing that all the stores would be closed, with the exception of the corner store and perhaps the local pharmacy. While I was mulling things over in my mind, the thought came to me that I should take him Communion. *Not a good idea*, I told myself. *Remember, Teresa told you that Pierre is an atheist.*

The voice inside my heart grew stronger, and the message was the same: *Take him Communion*. When I had approached the altar to receive, I requested a second host from the priest, and he placed it in my hand. I wrapped it carefully in a tissue that I had taken from my purse. When the Mass ended, I left the church and walked with reverence the two blocks to Pierre and Teresa's home, knowing that I was carrying a special gift from "the Father" to a father.

I knew they would not be expecting me that day, so I approached the door with trepidation and gave a gentle knock. Teresa who seemed pleased to see me was standing at the open door. "You were sent," she said.

I was not sure what she meant by the comment, so I blurted out that, since it was Father's Day, I had a gift for Pierre. She could take part if she wished. I then followed Teresa into Pierre's room and was somewhat surprised, but pleased, to see him sitting up in his bed. He looked no different than he had the previous Tuesday. *It was just a dream*, I told myself. *He looks great*. Teresa explained that I had brought him Communion, and Pierre reacted with a shy smile.

I walked over and stood by the left side of his bed, while Teresa took her place to his right. She asked if I would recite the Lord's Prayer in French with Pierre while she prayed in Spanish. I held the host in my open hand for all to see, and when we began to pray, an incredible sense of peace and tranquility filled every corner of the room. It was all very surreal, and I had to fight back the tears that welled up in my eyes.

After we had finished our prayers, I offered the host to Pierre with the words "the body of Christ." When he held out his hand in acceptance, I knew at that very moment that Pierre understood the meaning of unconditional love. I left the room quietly, and on my walk home, I tried to absorb all that had just taken place.

Later that evening I was sad when I heard that Pierre had been taken to the hospital. On Monday morning, I stopped by and was happy to find him in good spirits. During our visit, Pierre told me how happy he was to see his daughter. I kidded him about getting home by Tuesday, because we had a standing date. Just as I was about to leave the room, Pierre reached up with his right hand, and in the same affectionate gesture I had witnessed in my dream, he tickled the tip of my nose. However, this was not a dream; it was real, and I recognized that what had just taken place was far greater than both of us could have imagined.

The next morning I received the news that Pierre had slipped away quietly just as the sun was trying to peek over the horizon, with Teresa and his daughter at his bedside.

After the funeral Mass, the mourners followed the procession out to the cemetery, a peaceful place situated on the side of a hill, with a view of the city in the distance. It was a beautiful Saturday morning, with not a cloud in sight. The birds were making their presence known over the rustle of the fresh green leaves on the elegant birch trees. We were a small group of mourners as we gathered around Teresa, listening to the sound of the guitar player. The lyrics to the song "Vaya con Dios" were being carried to her by the soft warm breeze of spring.

It was hard to believe that a mere six weeks had passed since I first met Pierre, and now I was standing at his graveside, comforting his widow, and wishing him well as his soul journeyed on to a place beyond my comprehension. Pierre's friend Claudio, who was standing next to me, said the stars were all aligned for him that day, and I had to agree that, indeed, they were.

I will never fully understand why I was chosen to be a part of that scene. However, I know with certainty that I feel gratitude for the privilege of having witnessed first-hand the power of God.

CHAPTER TEN

Full Circle

This story is about a little girl who spent part of her childhood in a rooming house in Charlo, a small community on the east coast of Canada. The building had one washroom that was shared by four families, not unusual in the fifties. Sarah was one of five children who knew no other way of life. She remembers when she was about eight years of age; she was walking to school one morning feeling hungry. She decided to stop at the drugstore and steal a chocolate bar. As a younger child, she had learned the art of stealing coal from neighbours' basements in order to keep warm.

The proprietor caught Sarah in the act and thought it was time to put a stop to the stealing that was going on behind his back. When he told Sarah that he was taking her to the police, she started to cry, but this did not dissuade the merchant from escorting her out of the store in search of a police officer. She recalls a local police officer standing at the corner in his uniform and shiny black boots. Sarah cried even harder as they approached the officer. The storeowner quickly explained the situation and left Sarah in the hands of the law.

The police officer knelt down on one knee beside Sarah and then asked her, "Why did you steal, little girl?"

"Because I was hungry," she replied through her sniffles.

"Why did you not eat at home?"

"We have no food," she replied. He then took her by the hand and walked to the soda shop across the street. His huge, gentle hand impressed her as it engulfed hers. His tall, slender frame made him look like a giant. As she stood beside him, her body was trembling.

The officer ordered breakfast for her, and she sat on the stool next to him. She quickly ate the toast and banana placed in front of her, and while she drank her juice, he talked about the dangers of stealing. He went on to explain that God sees everything that we do. He then told her that stealing was wrong and that each time we steal it hurts God.

After Sarah had finished her breakfast and promised the officer never to steal again, she headed off to school. She had made sure not to divulge where she lived nor the state of her home life. The rule was never to tell family secrets, or the children might be taken away from their parents.

As the years sped by, the memories of that day soon faded from her mind. Her father was in his early forties when he passed away. Sarah's mother and older brother would now have to find work in order to support the family. It meant many moves to different communities just to survive.

Sarah faced many difficulties growing up, but her resilience never failed. She often sought refuge in the church, where she would talk to God. Years later, she became a nurse and married a military man. They travelled to many parts of our country and abroad, spending several years in Germany. After raising two young boys, and now in her late forties, she returned to her beloved east coast and bought a home about 100 miles from where she had grown up.

After moving into her new home, she soon found work. Her new job would give her the opportunity to work in the community, and Sarah felt up to the challenges and was excited at the thoughts of the wonderful people she would meet. Her love of people shone through her personality and her career as a nurse.

Sarah soon settled into the area and her work. She had a hard time referring to it as work, as she loved helping people and often went over and above the call of duty. She would usually call ahead to let clients know that she was on her way and would soon be arriving at their home.

This day she was coming to her last client. Shortly after making the phone call, she arrived at the home of an elderly patient. This was a new client, and she looked forward to the meeting. She rang the doorbell to his apartment, and a rather frail-looking man in his late eighties answered the door. His body was hunched over, and when he held out his hand, the hair at the back of her neck stood up, but she could not understand why. He greeted her warmly and offered to make tea. She followed him into the living room and sat on the sofa, while he disappeared into the kitchen.

As Sarah's eyes wandered around the room, she noticed a crucifix on the wall in front of her, and beside it was a picture of a man in a police uniform. She walked over to read the inscription at the bottom of the picture. Suddenly, Sarah could not believe her eyes. She now understood why seeing this stranger had stirred something inside her. The old man in the kitchen was the police officer who had changed the course of her life, and memories of that day long ago came back to her.

When he returned to the living room with the teapot, he found Sarah crying. "Why are you crying, dear?" he asked. "You seem so upset; please come and sit down."

Sarah walked over to the couch before asking him, "Do you remember when you were a young police officer in Charlo, about forty-five years ago?"

"Yes," he replied, "of course I do."

"Do you remember buying breakfast for a little girl who had stolen a chocolate bar?"

"Are you that little girl?" he asked his voice now filled with emotion.

"Yes, I am," she replied through her tears.

"When you were hungry, I was able to nourish you," he said, "and now that I am dying, you have come to care for me." The old man was very happy to meet her again and sang praises to God for this wonderful encounter. For the next hour, with teacups in hand, they talked about their lives, and Sarah learned that the man had retired as police chief several years earlier. He had left his community after his wife had passed away and was now living with his daughter.

Sarah cared for the dear man for approximately two months, and on one visit, he asked her if she could do him a favour. "What is that?" she asked.

"When I am gone, would you go to my funeral service and share our story with my friends and colleagues?" He wanted them all to know that whatever you do in this life, be it an act of kindness or otherwise, will always come back to find you. In his case, it had taken forty-five years to come full circle, and it had been worth the wait. Sarah agreed to carry out his wishes.

What a blessing that the old man and the young woman should meet again after all those years, allowing him to be witness once more to the love of God!

CHAPTER ELEVEN

Sophie and Her Courageous Battle with Cancer Saying Goodbye

We had met twenty-eight years ago in a small town in Northern Canada. She was working as a nurse and had been for many years. I was a nursing student at the time. We quickly became good friends.

Her friendly, warm personality and great sense of humour were her drawing card. I have never met a Maritimer I did not like, and Sophie was no exception. If you have ever visited the East Coast, you know what I mean.

Sophie grew up on the outskirts of Moncton. She was one of four children. Her dad was a farmer, and Sophie was the tomboy of the family. When I first met Grace, I could hardly believe that she was Sophie's sister, let alone her twin. Sophie was tall and slim, like their dad. Grace was petite, like their mother. They did share similar characteristics, though. Both girls were nurses and both were kind, caring women, but they had very different interests and lifestyles. Grace loved nice clothing, fine jewellery, good china, and travel. Sophie loved blue jeans, fishing rods, white rum, and 7-Up. Her best and happiest times were sitting by a lake, watching ducks along the shoreline, cooking over an open fire, or listening to country music in the company of friends. I can still hear her saying, "That was a bit of fun."

When I first met Sophie, she had already undergone a hysterectomy because of abnormal uterine cells. Several years later, she had surgery for breast cancer, and now she was facing leukemia. Twice divorced, but Sophie felt that she had had a good life. Sophie maintained a positive attitude. If she felt down, she got over it rather quickly. Self-pity was not in her makeup. She just wanted to get on with life.

In July of 2007 Jasmine, Gwen, and I travelled from different provinces to visit our dear friend who was now living in eastern Canada. Sophie had arranged for the three of us to rent a cottage close to the hospital. She was just recovering from a series of treatments. Each day started with a short time at her bedside. It did not matter that she could not accompany us on our day trips. She was happy to hear about our adventures, and in the evening, we would stop in for a short visit and bid her goodnight. Whether we had been out eating lobster—her treat—or sightseeing, she wanted to hear all the details and loved to laugh at our antics. She was given a four-hour pass during our visit, and we enjoyed the time at her apartment.

One afternoon we arranged a private party at the hospital. She was pleased when we arrived wearing matching kerchiefs and bringing one for her. We ordered in her favourite meal, Chinese food. We had purchased the fine Chinet plates at the local shopping centre, and I had found a new tablecloth in the trunk of her car, on which she commented and then laughed when we told her it was hers. She had planned to return it for a refund. It was a special day, one we would all cherish. She looked so weak, her hair all gone from the chemotherapy, but her zest for life still shone through her beautiful brown eyes.

When we left New Brunswick a week later, we were not sure we would see Sophie again. We had arranged to leave from the hospital that morning, and her friend Tom had offered to take us to the airport. We were all waiting at the front door, with Sophie in a wheelchair. Tom pulled up in his motor home and invited us in for coffee and doughnuts. How thoughtful he was! We sat in the hospital parking lot and shared a few more laughs before saying our goodbyes.

It was a quiet trip to the airport, each of us filled with our own thoughts. Later that year I flew to Halifax and was able to spend a few more hours with Sophie.

That fall, Sophie made the trip to Nova Scotia, where she would undergo tests for a possible stem cell transplant. She hoped to put an end to this disease. She later returned for the transplant in the company of her twin. Grace remained there for weeks and rarely left her bedside.

The months following the transplant were difficult. The complications were many, and her situation was often critical, but she fought hard.

Sophie had met many wonderful people along the way. Her friend Tom was one of these people. He was a widower who for the second time would have to watch someone he loved suffer through the pains of cancer. He travelled to Halifax shortly after her transplant and remained there until she was able to return home. Twice a day he would walk from his motel room and sit at her bedside.

Sophie was placed in reverse isolation, as her immune system was very fragile. Each time Tom entered her room she would be wearing a long-sleeved hospital gown, a mask, and gloves, and he would have to do the same. This went on for months, but he remained by her side. He had promised that he would not return home without her, and he was a man of his word.

After she returned home in the spring of 2008, Sophie was in and out of the hospital many times for more treatments, but the leukemia would not go away. She did manage to get home for a couple of weeks and enjoy a few outings with Tom. They had a special place where Tom would park his motor home and Sophie could watch the ducks on the water. She loved the simple things in life. They brought her the most joy. She had that right.

I spoke to Sophie the day she went back to the hospital. Her voice was weak, and I cried when I hung up the phone. I knew that I had just said goodbye to my dear friend.

I called the hospital the next day, hoping to hear her voice once more. There was no telephone in her room. As a distraction, I decided to look through my blanket box. I was hoping to find a certain birthday card that Mom had sent to my son years earlier. I searched in vain. While I was flipping through some papers, I came across a poem that Sophie had sent me on October 19, 1992. It was now October 18, 2008. I could not remember the significance of her sending it to me. When I read the poem for the second time, I understood the message.

To my dear friend Jane,

God hath not promised skies always blue,
Flower-strewn pathways all our lives through;
God hath not promised sun without rain,
Joy without sorrow, peace without pain.

But God hath promised strength for the day,
Rest for the labour, light for the way,
Grace for the trials, help from above,
Unfailing sympathy, undying love.

Love, Sophie
(Taken from a hymn, "What God Hath Promised," by Annie Johnson Flint, 1919.)

A coincidence? I do not believe so. Later that evening I called Grace and when I told her about the poem, she asked if I could send it by e-mail. The next morning, October 19, 2008, sixteen years after receiving the poem, Grace delivered it to Sophie. It read "To my dear friend Sophie . . . Love, Jane."

On October 22, Sophie's condition worsened. She was not responsive, so her sister decided to spend the night. Tom left, with plans to return the following morning. Later that evening, Sophie showed signs of restlessness, and Grace asked for medication to make her comfortable.

"I decided to lie in bed beside her," she told me later. "I spoke to her in a soft voice, and I let her know that she was free to go. Family would be waiting for her on the other side. A short time later, Sophie opened her eyes wide and looked beyond the room. At that moment, I realized that she knew where she was going."

Just after midnight on October 23, Sophie slipped quietly from this world. Grace lay beside her twin, grateful for the moment they had shared. It was a gift from her sister that she would always keep close to her heart. They had come into the world together, and now Sophie was gone. She had taken a part of Grace with her, and in so doing, she had left a part of herself behind.

This story is dedicated to our dear friend Sophie, who showed courage, faith, hope, and love in the face of life and death.
Love,
Jane, Jasmine, and Gwen

CHAPTER TWELVE

Remember Me

"Remember me." Those two words take me back to my childhood. They are a reminder of two special people who brought a lot of joy to our family, an aunt and uncle who had both earned and deserved the title of grandparent. Both my grandmothers and Dad's father had passed away before I was born, and Mom's father relocated to Ontario and moved in with his eldest son after Grandma died. Aunt Lise and Uncle Omer filled the grandparent role very well. All the attributes that we associate with a loving grandfather and grandmother belonged to them. They could not have loved us more.

Dad's sister and her husband were truly a blessing in our lives. My uncle had served in the Second World War in Italy, and after the war, he had met and married my Aunt Lise, a widow who never had children of her own. We remember hearing rumblings from the adult world about war, but our uncle could never bring himself to talk about it.

We lived next door to these beautiful people for many years, and I can still smell the aroma of fresh-baked bread as I walked by Auntie's house. We were always welcome to stop in for a treat, and we often did. Aunt Lise was a very tiny woman. Her hair was worn in a tight perm, and she could always be seen in a freshly laundered housedress. Our uncle was an ordinary man of small stature with a quiet disposition, who had a passion for fishing.

Auntie enjoyed getting together with family and friends, and she loved to sing. One of her favourite songs, which was recorded in 1962, was "Remember Me" by Johnny Burnette. She sang it often.

These two people exemplified the meanings of *kind* and *generous*. The house they lived in was half of a duplex owned by the power plant. They never accumulated much in their lifetime, as they gave away most of what they had. Uncle had a steady job at the plant, so they were able to purchase the first television in our small community. During the summers, our friends and cousins would gather at their home. It was a weekly event where we would all enjoy a movie, followed by juice and cookies. We filled their small living room, and they were always happy to have us. It was quite an event experiencing television for the first time.

Our family then lived on the outskirts of the community. It was a twenty-minute walk through the woods to their house. So, on movie night, we would head down the path with our older brother Andrew. He was about nine years old at the time and in charge of the lantern for our return trip home. On our way back, I was always so frightened that I would vow never to return. The darkness was all-encompassing, and my imagination would always get the better of me. I was certain that a bobcat or other wild animal would be waiting to attack us from the dense trees that lined the path. It never happened, and in the light of day, my fears were soon forgotten. The following week, we would once again head down the road for another night at the movies.

Electrical storms were another experience that left an imprint on my siblings and me. We learned from our Uncle Omer about the safety of rubber. During a thunderstorm, our uncle would go to his garage and sit in his car. I have no recollection of seeing him drive his car, but he did sit in it often. My dad did not own a vehicle at the time, so this was not an option for us. Because we lived in close proximity to the power plant, the electrical storms were wicked and could last for hours. If there was a storm during the night, our parents would wake us up out of a sound sleep, and we would make our way down the stairs to the living room. They were concerned about the possibility of lightning striking the house and them not being able to get us out in time. When we were all accounted for, Mom would retrieve the bottle of holy water from the top of the cookstove and bless each one of us. Half asleep, and by the light of the coal oil lamp, we would then rummage around the house in search of our boots. While we sat around in pyjamas and the safety of our rubber boots and waited for the storm to pass, it was a time of prayer. When the storm ended, our rubber boots off, we would return to the comfort of our beds and a few more hours of sleep. There were many storms in the area, and by the end of summer, we had the routine down pat.

Many of our Christmases were made extra special by the generosity of our aunt and uncle. Years later, we learned that they were largely responsible for our shrieks of joy on Christmas mornings.

Our Uncle Omer also introduced us to pasta and garlic. He had learned to cook while in Italy, and he was happy to show off his skills. We sure enjoyed it when he would arrive at our door with the necessary ingredients and cook up a large pot of spaghetti.

He worked as a night watchman at the power plant, and on his way home, he would often stop by the house with a salmon he had taken out of the pond in the early hours of the morning. I can still hear his voice as he came through the back door. "Here, Rose, cook this up for the kids." Mom was grateful, because she had many hungry mouths to feed.

When we got older, we had to be careful not to compliment our aunt about anything she was wearing or had in her home. If we did, she would want us to take it. It could be the sweater that she was wearing or the glass dish on the table. Aunt Lise loved us and enjoyed bragging to strangers that we were her brother's kids.

Each year on Remembrance Day, Aunt Lise and Uncle Omer would get together with the neighbours and celebrate their freedom. They honoured the men and women who had fought for their countries. I remember one year as being different.

That year, Aunt Lise joined family and friends for the Remembrance Day celebration. Uncle had to work the evening shift. When he returned around midnight, he was shocked to find Auntie slumped over in her rocking chair. He carried her body to the sofa, but she did not recover. Her death at the age of 73 was the result of a fatal heart attack. On Remembrance Day, November 11 each year, as a tribute to these beautiful people, I sing the first verse of the song I heard so often during my childhood: "Remember me; I'm the one who loves you." It always makes me smile.

We wondered how our uncle would manage without our aunt. He was a very quiet man who mostly kept to himself. Eventually Uncle Omer moved away from the community they had called home for some forty years and found some peace at his brother's cottage. That is where he lived out the remainder of his life, enjoying the solitude, with his fishing rod at his side. I remember them both with a thankful heart for their love and their dedication to our family.

They have left us with many memories—memories of the injustice and pain of war that can still be felt throughout the world today, memories found in the simple joys of everyday living, fond memories of our childhood, and memories of their love and generosity, the memories that taught us about the joy of giving to others. Each year I make my way to the cenotaph where the community gathers to honour the people like my uncle, who fought so that we might enjoy our freedom.

As I look back on my life, I cannot help but feel an incredible sense of gratitude for the many blessings I have received. Looking at the suffering people in the world today, I realize that the gift of being raised with very little luxury has allowed me to recognize that I have had a privileged life. The gifts of faith, love, and gratitude were constant during my childhood. My parents, grandparents, and extended family taught and reflected God's love and mercy. They taught us to appreciate what little we did have but also, perhaps more importantly, the joy of sharing with others. When I get out of bed each morning and look out my window at nature and its constantly changing pictures, I reflect, pause, and give thanks to the One who loves me.

IN CONCLUSION

I want to thank the friends and family who have contributed to these stories. It is a gift and a privilege for me to put them down on paper and share them with you. We have all heard or read stories similar to these, and they have left us wondering about life and the mystery that it holds for each of us. We often tend to neglect or ignore the quiet promptings of our inner voices. Whenever I open my heart to not only receive the messages but also to act upon them, wonderful things happen, leaving me with a renewed sense of well-being. As human beings, we must remember that, regardless of our race, colour, orientation, or belief, it is the respect and love we share with one another that will ultimately make our world a better place for those who will follow.

**Mom's 80th birthday celebration
Top row, left to right: Theresa, Marie, Evelyn,
Blanche (author), Andrew, Eddy, Roy, Edward,
Tina behind Mom and Jackie**

ABOUT THE AUTHOR

Blanche Jeannine Brideau, born in Canada of Acadian descent, grew up in a small town in northern New Brunswick as the sixth of twelve children. At the age of seventeen, she headed for Ontario with her friend Louise. Several years later, she travelled to the Northwest Territories with her husband and young son, where she worked in the health field. Experiences during her career as a nurse gave her many opportunities to see God's hand at work. The idea to write a collection of short stories came to her from a stranger's suggestion during her return flight home after her mother's death. That encounter allowed her to recognize and experience God's overwhelming generosity. In 1998, she left the North and is now living in Brighton, Ontario, with her husband, Patrick, and their dog, Tess, where she continues to write and volunteer in her community.